Vowels
with
Vitality

Practicing Long and Short Vowels

Cheryl Callighan

Good Year Books
Parsippany, New Jersey

This book is dedicated to Paul, Bryce, and Shaun for all their loving support.

Good Year Books

are available for most basic curriculum subjects plus many enrichment areas. For more Good Year Books, contact your local bookseller or educational dealer. For a complete catalog with information about other Good Year Books, please write:

Good Year Books
An imprint of Pearson Learning
299 Jefferson Road, P.O. Box 480
Parsippany, NJ 07054-0480

www.pearsonlearning.com

1-800-321-3106

Illustrations: Jamie Smith
Book Design: M. Jane Heelan
Design Manager: M. Jane Heelan
Executive Editor: Judith Adams

ISBN 0-673-59256-1

1 2 3 4 5 6 7 8 9 - ML - 06 05 04 03 02 01 00

This Book Is Printed
On Recycled Paper

TABLE OF CONTENTS

INTRODUCTION

Phonics

Phonics is the study of the relationship between sounds and letters. Debates about the value of phonics instruction and the appropriate emphasis on phonics in reading programs have raged for decades. These days, most educators accept phonics—along with other strategies, such as learning sight words and using context clues—as an essential component of effective reading and spelling programs.

The vowel sounds are generally taught after the single consonant sounds have been mastered. This book assumes that children know all the single consonant sounds.

Every syllable of every word in English has a vowel or vowel sound. Unfortunately, English does not play fair when it comes to vowels. A vowel does not always have the same sound. Each vowel has both a long and a short sound. When vowels are next to each other in words, new sounds may occur. In words, surrounding consonants, such as *l* and *r*, may change vowel sounds. To add to the confusion, the consonants *y* and *w* sometimes function as vowels.

Sounds and Focus Words in <u>Vowels with Vitality</u>

This book emphasizes long and short vowel sounds but includes other common vowel sounds as well. The focus words were selected from several sources: Fry New Instant Word List—300 words that comprise 65 percent of elementary written material (Edward Fry, *The Reading Teacher*, 1980); High Utility 500—the 500 most frequently used words in children's writing (C.B. Smith and G. M. Ingersoll, *Written Vocabulary of Elementary School Pupils*, 1984); and *The American Heritage Word Frequency Study* (Carroll, Davies, Richman, 1993). Words that follow the same phonics patterns as words on these lists are also included.

The reliability of phonics generalizations was considered, and target words with the most reliable patterns appear in this book. These patterns include CVC, CVC silent *e*, two vowels together giving the first vowel the long sound, and *r*-controlled vowels.

Learning Styles

Appealing to children's unique learning styles can make the

sometimes daunting task of teaching phonics generalizations to young children easier. These learning styles fall into three major categories: auditory, visual, and tactile. Children are often aware of the style they prefer. A child may say, *I learn a lot by listening* or *I understand better if I can see something.* Of course, no child fits perfectly into only one category. Most children learn well from varied activities that tap into all three learning styles. Here are some behavior cues to help you determine the dominant learning styles of your students.

Auditory learners

- gain understanding better by listening than reading
- learn well from songs
- enjoy small-group discussions
- are usually good listeners
- follow oral directions well
- enjoy making oral presentations
- may hum or talk frequently while working
- learn phonics generalizations better if they pronounce the sounds
- enjoy listening to lessons on audio tape
- have difficulty reading long assignments silently
- prefer studying with background music
- may have sophisticated vocabularies

Visual learners

- learn well by reading silently
- grasp information easily from charts, maps, and graphs
- need to see written directions
- often learn phonics by associating sounds with pictures
- may learn well from videos
- are stimulated by colorful presentations
- often like to doodle
- usually like quiet work environments
- recognize word patterns easily
- may rely heavily on illustrations to aid comprehension
- often have trouble processing information presented orally
- may think and visualize concepts before attempting an activity

Tactile learners

- understand stories better if they act them out
- learn well using manipulatives
- enjoy body movement activities
- can master difficult concepts through texture associations
- often have excellent mechanical skills
- enjoy lying on the floor or being wedged under a desk as they work
- often plunge into activities before directions are given
- may excel at problem solving

- may exhibit repetitive mannerisms, such as finger drumming, foot tapping, and hair twisting as they work

Features in Vowels with Vitality

- Activities—games, projects, and lessons that reinforce vowel sounds and decoding skills.
- Skits—short plays, each of which introduces a concept and includes a worksheet.

- Reproducible Worksheets— coloring activities and skill sheets that let you choose vowel sounds to practice and review.
- Word Lists—words categorized by vowel sounds to use in projects and activities.

A Vowel Primer

The variations in pronunciation of vowels are numerous and can be puzzling. Following is a quick reference guide to the vowel sounds.

Short Vowels

Short *a* —*add, can, hatch, past, rack, tag*

Short *e* —*bed, check, egg, left, set, ten*

Short *i* —*bridge, ink, mix, pick, ring, witch*

Short *o* —*box, dog, frog, knob, off, pond*

> Some programs include the sound of short *o* in *dog* and *soft*. Other programs limit short *o* to the sound in *hot*. The activities in this book take the former approach.

Short *u* —*brush, cup, hug, plum, punch, truck*

Long Vowels

Long *a* —*bake, day, lace, pail, rain, stage*

Long *e* —*beach, cheese, eve, key, seal, three*

Long *i* —*bike, die, mine, pipe, rise, tried*

> The letter *y* often yields this long vowel sound, as in *my, rhyme, spy, type*. This book includes these words under long *i*.

Long *o* —*go, bone, dome, hole, joke, rope*

> Many educators also place the vowel digraph *ow*, as in *blow, crow, grow, slow*, in this category.

Long *u* —*blue, cute, fuse, huge, rude, tube*

> Long *u* appears in many other combinations. The pairing of *e* and *w* yields *few, grew, stew, view*. Single *o* gives us the long *u* sound in *do*. A combination of *o* and *u* provides the long *u* sound in *you* and *youth*. These miscellaneous spellings will be included with the long *u* lessons in this book.

R-Controlled Vowels

Pairing vowels with the letter *r* creates an entirely new set of sounds known as *r*-controlled vowels.

> *ar* —*arm, dark, hard, jar, smart, starch*
>
> *er* —*fern, germ, her, perch, serve, verb*
>
> *ir* —*bird, chirp, dirt, firm, sir, third*
>
> *or* —*born, cord, for, more, port, stork*
>
> *ur* —*burn, curb, fur, hurt, surf, urge*

Miscellaneous Vowel Sounds

aw — *bawl, claw, hawk, lawn, saw*

> The vowel combination *a* and *w* is often taught along with *au,* since *aw* and *au* yield the same sound.

ow — *brown, cow, now, prowl / show, grow, flow*

> Context clues generally provide the best way to teach the difference between *ow* in *down* and *ow* in *blown.*

Teachers need to be aware that regional dialects will affect the pronunciation of, mastery of, and ability to discriminate some vowel sounds. Be sensitive to these speech variations. Students with English as a second language will also need special attention for vowel mastery.

Activities

The following pages contain organized activities for children to do, either as a class, in small groups, or in pairs. The activities give children an opportunity to practice and apply what they are learning about long and short vowels. They are intended as practice or enrichment—a supplement to your school's reading and spelling curricula. You should follow the guidelines set down by your current programs, which may require you to modify some of the activities.

Each activity page consists of a list of the materials required for the activity, teacher preparation instructions when necessary, and the procedure for children to follow. The page also indicates which learning styles children use in the activity: tactile, visual, and/or auditory. Children most easily learn concepts presented in their dominant learning style, but lessons that elicit their less dominant learning styles help them develop other ways to learn.

When an activity calls for you to provide words using long or short vowel sounds, you may refer to the list of such words at the back of the book.

Vowel Shape Posters

This activity helps teach and reinforce long and short vowel sounds. Vowel shape posters provide a ready reference for vowel sounds throughout the school year.

Materials

poster board or heavy
   construction paper
scissors
marker

Preparation

1. Draw and cut out shapes for the items listed below:

hat—short *a*	whale—long *a*
egg—short *e*	tree—long *e*
fish—short *i*	kite—long *i*
sock—short *o*	boat—long *o*
bus—short *u*	cube—long *u*

   Make the shapes large enough to accommodate lists of words.

2. Label the top of each shape with its vowel sound. (For example, the cutout of a cube will be labeled "long *u*.")

Procedure

1. Introduce one vowel sound and its corresponding shape poster at each session. Show the class the cutout and say the word it represents. Explain that words that rhyme with this word all have the same vowel sound. As an example, words that rhyme with *kite* might include *bite, night,* and so on. Ask children to think of such rhyming words. Print the words children suggest on the poster.

2. Read the words on the poster with the class. Display the poster so that children can refer to it later.

3. Repeat this procedure as you introduce or reinforce other vowel sounds. Children can add words to the posters during the year.

Word Pattern Books

Materials

poster board
scissors
construction paper
markers or crayons
stapler

To make word pattern books, children add letters to word patterns to form words.

Preparation

1. Cut the poster board into 2-by-6-inch rectangles. Make one rectangle for each child. You can create extra rectangles to make pattern books for upcoming lessons.

2. Cut the construction paper into 2-inch squares. You will need 6 to 10 squares for each child.

3. Write a word pattern on each poster board rectangle, aligned to the right. Here are some suggested word patterns:

at	en	in	ot	ub
and	et	it	op	ug
an	ell	ill	od	up
ap	ent	itch	og	un
ack	end	ix	ock	ut
ash	est	ish		ump
ast	elt			unch
ay	eel	ime	oad	ube
ate	eat	ine	old	ute
ale	eed	ike	one	
ain	ee	ile	oat	
ake	ea	ight		
ame	eam	ice		
		ind		

Procedure

1. Give each child a poster board rectangle and a supply of construction paper squares. Tell children to look at the word pattern on the rectangle. Ask them to identify the vowel sound in the pattern. Ask them to think of words with this pattern.

2. Show children how to write one or two letters on a square and place the square at the left of a word pattern rectangle to form a word.

3. Challenge children to make as many words as they can. Help children staple their stacks of squares to the rectangles to make word pattern books.

4. Have children share their pattern books with one another. Save the books so that children can use them to review word patterns.

Fuzzy Vowels

Children write words and reinforce the long, short, and silent vowels by outlining the vowels with yarn.

Materials

- about 10 medium paper grocery bags
- scissors
- red, green, and black yarn
- three containers
- glue
- markers or crayons

Preparation

1. Cut the bottoms off the bags. Cut each bag along one side and lay it flat. Cut each bag into three or four equal-size rectangles.

2. Cut the yarn into 4-inch lengths. You will need 5 to 10 pieces of each color for each child. Place the yarn pieces into three containers, separated by color. Label the container with the red yarn *Short,* the one with the green yarn *Long,* and the one with the black yarn *Silent.*

3. Make sure the glue, scissors, markers or crayons, and yarn are within easy reach of the children.

Procedure

1. Give each child a paper rectangle.

2. On the board or overhead, list 5 to 10 words containing long or short vowels from the word list in the back of this book. Tell children to use markers or crayons to write the words in large letters on the rectangles.

3. Direct children to use the yarn to cover the vowels on the rectangles as follows: If a vowel in the word has a short sound, use red yarn; if a vowel has a long sound, use green; if a vowel is silent, use black. After children practice forming the letters with the yarn, they can glue the yarn to the paper. You may wish to prepare some sample rectangles in advance, with yarn already in place, to demonstrate the concept.

4. Display the completed words around the classroom.

Swirl-a-Word

As children trace shapes and pronounce words, they reinforce their knowledge of various word patterns.

Materials

crayons
drawing paper

Preparation

Write on the board pairs of words that change from a short vowel sound to a long vowel sound with the addition of a final e. Here are some suggested word pairs:

can	cane	bit	bite	hop	hope	cub	cube
fat	fate	dim	dime	mop	mope	cut	cute
hat	hate	fin	fine	not	note	dud	dude
mad	made	hid	hide	rob	robe	hug	huge
man	mane	kit	kite	rod	rode	tub	tube
mat	mate	pin	pine	tot	tote	us	use
pal	pale	rid	ride				
pan	pane	slid	slide				
rat	rate	slim	slime				
tap	tape						

Procedure

1. Divide the class into pairs and give paper to each pair. Ask children to use the crayons to print pairs of words, copied from the board, on their papers. Have children leave lots of space between the two words.

2. Have children say each word in the first pair out loud. Then have them trace outlines around each word, following the shape of the letters. Children should enlarge each outline slightly and then enlarge again at least three times. Outlines may overlap to make interesting patterns.

3. Children can continue in the same way with the other word pairs.

Keyboarding

Children review vowel sounds by "typing" words on illustrations of computer keyboards.

Materials

photocopies of page 19
crayons in five different
colors

Preparation

Make enough photocopies of the keyboards so that each child can have one. Cut each copy in half to make two keyboards. You can laminate the keyboards for longer use.

Procedure

1. Give each child a keyboard. Remind the class that the letters on a keyboard are not in alphabetical order.

2. Have children locate the letter A on the keyboard. Ask them to color this key, using a light-colored crayon so that the letter is still legible. (If the keyboards are laminated, children may need to use darker crayons.)

3. Ask a volunteer to name a word with the short *a* sound. Then spell the word very slowly. Tell children to touch each letter on the keyboard as the word is spelled.

4. Choose another short *a* word and continue in this manner.

5. Review as many words and vowel sounds as you like. Each time you focus on a new vowel sound, begin by having children color that vowel on the keyboard in a new color.

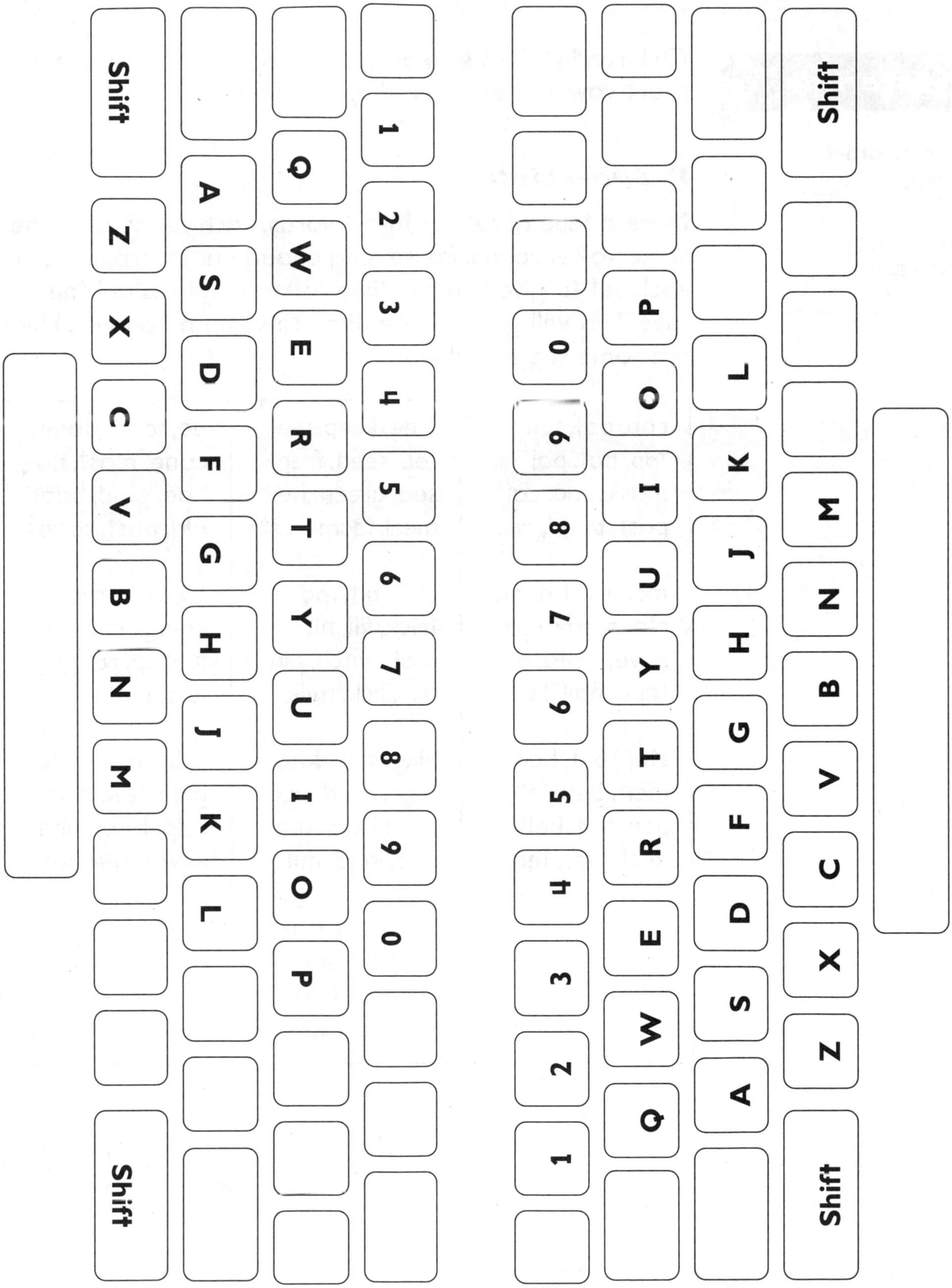
1 2 3 4 5 6 7 8 9 0
Q W E R T Y U I O P
A S D F G H J K L
Shift Z X C V B N M Shift
1 2 3 4 5 6 7 8 9 0
Q W E R T Y U I O P
A S D F G H J K L
Shift Z X C V B N M Shift

Do You Hear What I Hear?

Children listen to sets of words and identify the long or short vowel sound shared by each set.

Materials

cassette recorder
blank tape
paper
pencils
writing paper

Preparation

Make a tape of sets of three words, each set sharing the same vowel sound. Pause long enough after pronouncing each set to give yourself time to stop and restart the tape. This will give children time to write an answer. Here are some suggested word sets:

cab, bat, fan tap, hat, pal mask, sad, cat past, band, cap	tree, keep, we tea, seed, free sea, green, he meal, team, east	go, foam, tone cone, most, no hoe, gold, boat old, post, road
make, tail, name place, say, rain save, state, day tape, hail, late	pick, bit, mix trick, fill, hit miss, witch, pin trip, lick, milk	cup, fun, rub stump, cut, sun fun, up, rough fuss, puff, nut
step, pet, hen melt, bed, let pen, net, belt nest, wet, ten	bike, sign, kite time, mind, rice pie, bite, slime rice, kind, mile	cube, use, mule glue, few, cute rule, fuse, tube new, mute, hue
	hot, dock, drop off, soft, dog shop, rod, top lot, rock, spot	

Procedure

1. Give writing paper to each child. Have children number their papers 1 through 10.

2. Tell the class, *I am going to play a tape for you. Listen very carefully. You will hear a group of three words. All three words have the same vowel sound. Decide which vowel sound you hear. Write that sound next to number 1 on your paper. Listen to the first group.* (Play the tape, stopping it after the first group of words.) *What sound did you hear? Be sure you write whether it makes a long or a short sound.*

3. Continue playing the tape until children have listened to 10 groups of words, or more, depending on their abilities and attention spans.

4. Rewind the tape so that children can listen to the sets of words again. Have children repeat the words out loud and help them to agree on the answers they have written down.

Word Relay Race

Materials

writing paper
pencil

This action game requires children to recall and write words with specified long and short vowel sounds.

Preparation

Draw three vertical lines to divide the board into four columns.

Procedure

1. Have the class form four teams and choose team names. Write each team's name on a section of the board. Make sure the members of each team can locate their team's section. You may wish to go over how to keep score by making tally marks by fives.

2. Have one player from each team go to the appropriate section of the board. Tell the children at the board that they are to write a word using the vowel sound you call out. Announce a vowel sound: for example, long *o*. The four children should write a word that has this sound. The first player to write a correct word receives two points for his or her team. All other correct answers receive one point.

3. Call the next player from each team. Continue until everyone has had a chance to participate.

4. Choose a volunteer from each group. Have the volunteers work together to add up the points and declare the winning team.

5. Have the class read all the correct words on the board aloud together.

Paper Chains

This favorite childhood activity calls for children to classify words by vowel sounds.

Materials

construction paper
markers
scissors
stapler or tape

Preparation

1. Cut the construction paper into narrow strips. You will need about 150 strips to start with, plus one more for each child in the class.

2. First, set aside enough blank strips so that each child can have one. Next, write a different word on each of the remaining strips. For each vowel sound there should be 15 words. Refer to the list at the back of this book for words to use. If you wish to involve the children at this stage, you can give them lists of words and ask them to write the words on the strips.

Procedure

1. Divide the class into four or five small groups. Pass out the same number of random word strips to each group.

2. Have the groups of children divide their word strips into vowel sound groups. Then direct children to form a paper chain out of each group of word strips by looping the strips together and stapling or taping them.

3. Work together with children to join each set of chains to form longer chains. When they are done, there should be 10 long chains, one for each long and short vowel sound.

4. Pass out one blank strip to each child. Have children use their blank strips to write a word containing one of the vowel sounds. Ask children to add their strips to the paper chains with the corresponding vowel sounds. Hang them up.

5. Encourage children to add words as they discover them during the year.

Dial-a-Word

Materials

scraps of colored paper
scissors
large paper plates
crayons or markers
brad fasteners

Children create letter dials that help them practice spelling words.

Preparation

Cut a 3-inch-long triangular pointer from the scrap paper for each child.

Procedure

1. Give each child a paper plate. Ask children to write the letters of the alphabet around the edge of the plate with *A* at the top and *M* at the bottom. *G* goes in the three o'clock position and *S* goes at nine o'clock. Have children circle the vowels.

2. Give each child a pointer. Help them attach the pointers to the center of each plate with a brad fastener to make a dial.

3. Demonstrate how to use the dials by holding one up and saying a word. Ask children to identify the vowel sound. Move the pointer to each letter on the dial as you slowly spell the word.

4. Have children use their dials as they spell several words with long and short vowel sounds. You can use words from the word list at the back of this book. Ask children to name the vowel sound in each word and to identify silent vowels. Save the dial-a-word devices to use again.

Vowels Can Be Wild!

In this game, children use dice as prompts for writing words with long and short vowel sounds.

Preparation

1. For game dice, you may use wooden or plastic cubes, soundless dice cut from large sponges, or large store-bought dice. Cover each face of each die with a blank sticker.

2. For each pair of dice, label the sides of one die *a, e, i, o, u,* and *WILD.* On the second die, mark three sides with the word *Long* and three sides with the word *Short.*

Procedure

1. Divide the class into small groups. Give each group a pair of dice.

2. Instruct children to play the game as follows:

   • The first player rolls the dice once and announces the combination: for example, long *a* or short *u.*

   • Each player in the group then writes a word using that vowel sound on a sheet of paper.

   • If the *WILD* side is showing, the child who rolled the dice may choose any long or short vowel to be used for that round. Play continues for the amount of time you specify.

3. At the end of the game, have children take turns reading their lists of words to the rest of their group. If you wish, you may then rotate the lists and ask children to continue reading until everyone has read all the words.

Picture Collages

Materials

large sheets of paper
pencils, crayons, or
    markers
scissors
glue
heavily illustrated
    magazines

Children create collages by choosing pictures of objects whose names contain long and short vowel sounds.

Preparation

This activity may be accomplished in two ways: Either the entire class works together to create 10 collages, or children work individually.

1. Label each large sheet with a vowel sound (*short a*, *long a*, *short* e, *long* e, and so on) and post the sheets around the classroom.

Procedure

1. Review the vowel sounds by asking volunteers to name one item for each vowel sound. (For example, when you name the vowel sound "short e" the class may say a word such as "leg.")

2. If you are doing the exercise as a class project, show children the large sheets of paper labeled with the vowel sounds. Invite children to look through the magazines. Tell them that when they find a picture they like of an object whose name contains a particular short or long vowel sound, they should cut out the picture and glue it to the sheet labeled with the corresponding vowel sound. Children should arrange the pictures on each sheet any way they like.

3. If children are making their own collages, have each child choose a vowel sound and write it at the top of his or her paper. Have children find pictures of objects whose names have the appropriate vowel sound, arrange them on the page, and glue them down.

4. Display the completed collages. Children will enjoy identifying the items they see pictured.

Magic Change Books

Children make word books to practice reading words with final silent e.

Preparation

1. Cut the poster board into 2-by-6-inch rectangles. You will need one rectangle for each child.

2. Cut the construction paper into 2-by-5-inch rectangles, 5 to 10 per child.

3. Write the words with short vowels from page 17 on the board.

Procedure

1. Have children work in pairs. Give each pair a poster board rectangle. Have children write a large e near the right edge.

2. Read the words from the board. Ask the class to say whether the type of vowel in the words is short or long. Ask what would happen if e were added to the ends of the words.

3. Give each pair of children 5 to 10 construction paper rectangles. Tell children to write one word from the board on each piece of paper.

4. Have children stack these rectangles on top of the poster board rectangle, with the construction paper rectangles aligned to the left. Help to staple them.

5. Ask children to write the letter e on the right side of the poster board rectangle.

6. Direct children to take turns, each reading words in their stack to their partner and then saying the word that is formed when a silent e is added.

Listen Up!

Children listen carefully to identify words whose vowel sounds differ from the others in a group.

Procedure

1. Tell children that they must listen very carefully to sets of words that you say. The first word will have the vowel sound that the other words in the set must match. If they hear a word or words in the set whose vowel sound differs from this word, they are to raise their hands.

2. Demonstrate the activity for the class, speaking clearly and pausing between each word. Say the words *bed, step, rest,* and *cup.* Children should raise their hands when they hear *cup.* If necessary, model again with other words.

3. Have children close their eyes.

4. Read each of the following sets of words.

   - add—bag, cell, ham, jack, latch
   - bench—bread, red, ship, knob
   - brick—chin, dig, clock, rich, fan, spit, witch
   - box—chop, shelf, sock, game, mop, odd, rock, mile
   - bug—cub, fudge, gull, mud, plug, pick, rug, shut, thumb
   - age—bake, lace, hat, skate, stage, tape, hope, slice, pail, name, dog
   - beans—team, meal, race, eve, deal, cheat, tap, eel, week, fish, steal
   - bike—bride, dime, flake, hide, ice, kite, bump, like, rice, shine, twice
   - bone—broke, close, rip, drove, hide, mole, poke, vase, robe, rode, zone
   - chute—crude, cup, cube, stack, dune, flute, make, fuse, huge, white, rule
   - aim—bail, chain, cab, fail, faith, dance, play, rat, pray, sad, stray, sail, trail, splash, tray

Quick Grab

This fast-paced game requires children to identify vowel sounds in words.

Preparation

1. Cut 10 to 15 index cards in half.

2. Choose 20 to 30 words from the word list at the back of the book. Write each word on a card half. You may use just short-vowel words, just long-vowel words, or a combination.

Procedure

1. To begin a game of Quick Grab, sit with a small group of children at a table or on the floor. Spread out the cards you prepared, printed side up.

2. Call out a clue that identifies one of the word cards. For example, you might say, *Find a word with a short* e *sound.* Children should look over the cards on the table and pick up the first one they find that matches the clue. The first player to pick up a correct card keeps it. If a player picks an incorrect word card, he or she must return one of the cards that he or she selected in a previous round to the table. Here are some possible clues:

   • Find a word with the same vowel sound as *pet.*
   • Find a word that has the short *u* sound.
   • Find a word that has a silent letter.
   • Find the word that rhymes with *job.*
   • Find a word that shows the rule *When two vowels go walking, the first does the talking.*

   You may also want to call out a clue that doesn't fit any of the cards.

3. When all the cards have been picked up, the player who has the most cards is the winner.

Wonderful Windsocks

Children follow step-by-step directions and classify vowel sounds to complete this art project.

Preparation

1. Cut construction paper into 6-by-18-inch rectangles. You will need one rectangle for each windsock.

2. Cut the crepe paper into streamers about 24 inches long. You will need five streamers for each windsock.

3. Make a sample windsock:

   • Label one of the rectangles either *Long Vowels* or *Short Vowels*. Use markers to make colorful designs.
   • Staple the rectangle to itself along its 6-inch length to form a short cylinder.

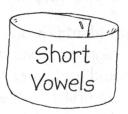

   • Staple five crepe paper streamers evenly spaced around the bottom of the cylinder.

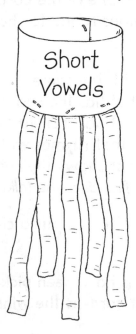

- Cut out five small pieces of construction paper. Write a different vowel on each piece of paper and glue the paper to a streamer.
- Cut out five more shapes. Draw a picture of an object or write a word with one of the five vowel sounds on each shape. Glue them to the cylinder. If you wrote *Long Vowels* on your construction paper, you should use objects or words with long vowel sounds; if you wrote *Short Vowels*, use objects or words with short vowel sounds.
- Punch two holes at the top of the cylinder on opposite sides. Thread yarn through the holes and knot it to make a loop so that the completed windsock can be hung up.

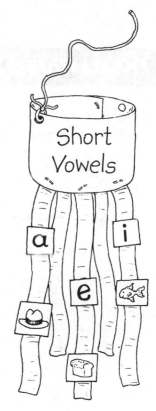

Procedure

1. Arrange the supplies in a spot convenient for the children.

2. Review long and short vowel sounds briefly. Let children choose either long or short vowels for their windsocks.

3. Pass out the rectangles and have children write *Long Vowels* or *Short Vowels* on them. Display the sample windsock and explain in detail how you made it.

4. Have children make their own windsocks according to the directions above. You can build in checkpoints to be sure that children are following the directions properly. For example, you may want to have children tell you which pictures they plan to draw on their construction-paper shapes to be sure that the pictures represent the proper sounds.

5. Hang the windsocks in the classroom for a cheerful display.

Quick Choice

Children play a fast-paced game in which they hold up colored paper flags to indicate whether they hear long or short vowel sounds in words.

Preparation

1. Cut the construction paper into 6-inch squares. You will need one green square and one red square for each child.

Procedure

1. Give each child a green square and a red square and explain that they will make flags to use in a vowel game. Ask children what vowel sounds they hear in the words *green* and *red*. Have children use a crayon or marker to write the word *Long* on the green square and write the word *Short* on the red square.

2. Have children place the flags on their desks in front of them. Tell the class you are going to read a word and that they are to decide if the word has a long or a short vowel sound. Instruct children to hold up their green flags if the word has a long vowel sound, and to hold up their red flags if the word has a short vowel sound. Using the word list at the back of this book, read a word to the class. Have children hold up the correct flag.

3. Continue to read words, checking to make sure children are answering correctly. Gradually increase the speed at which you read the words.

4. You can vary the game by choosing groups of children to respond: for example, children whose first names begin with *S, T,* and *R,* children sitting in the second row, children with brown eyes, children wearing an item of clothing with buttons, children with shoes that tie, and so on.

Pattern Poems

In this activity, children listen to and write poems with AABB rhyme schemes, using words with long and short vowel sounds.

Preparation

Find several simple rhyming poems whose rhyming words have one syllable and long or short vowel sounds. Mark the pages so that you can find them later.

Procedure

1. Read the poems to the class. Ask children to identify the rhyming words. Write these words on the board and point out the vowels.

2. Write the following poem on the board:

   There once was a red fox
   Who lived in a big box.
   This fox really liked to eat.
   His favorite dish was chicken meat.

3. Have a volunteer identify the rhyming words in the first two lines and name the vowel sound they share (short o). Label these lines A and A. Ask a second volunteer to find the rhyming words in the third and fourth lines and identify the vowel sound they share (long e). Label these lines B and B. Explain to the children that this rhyme scheme is called AABB.

4. Invite children to write poems with the AABB rhyme scheme, using rhyming words with long and short vowel sounds.

5. Have children underline the rhyming words in the first two lines of their poems (the A lines) and circle the rhyming words in the last two lines (the B lines).

6. Post the completed poems around the classroom.

Word Lines

In this word-making game, children review short vowel sounds.

Preparation

1. You will need 20 to 40 index cards for each small group. Use a black marker to draw a diagonal line bisecting each card.

2. On the left side of the card, use a blue marker to write a short vowel and a consonant from the first list below. Use a red marker to write a consonant from the second list on the right side of the card.

Vowel-consonant pairs: ad, ag, an, ap, at, eg, en, et, ig, in, ip, it, od, og, op, ot, ub, ug, un, ut; Consonants: b, c, d, f, g, h, j, l, m, n, p, r, s, t, w

Procedure

1. Give small groups 20 to 40 randomly chosen cards each.

2. Tell children that they will play a game as follows:

   • First the dealer deals the cards to the players.
   • The first player puts down a card faceup.
   • The next player tries to form a word by adding a card to the right or left of the card on the table, as shown below. If the player makes a word, he or she reads the word aloud.
   • Each time a player puts down a card, players read all the words in the line. Players who can't make words pass.
   • The first player with no cards wins.
   • For a cooperative game, group members work together to complete as long a word line as possible.

ad	m	ap	h	ot	p	en	s	at	w	in	c	an	j	et	r

Phonics Puzzles

Children use color-coded jigsaw puzzles to review long and short vowel sounds and write words with each sound.

Materials

10 different colors of construction paper
chalk in the same 10 colors (optional)
scissors
markers
envelopes
stickers

Preparation

1. On the board or overhead, write a key with 10 colors, each standing for a vowel sound. You can either use 10 different colors of chalk, or simply write the names of the colors. Suggestions: light blue—long *a*; pink—short *a*; green—long *e*; red—short *e*; brown—long *i*; gray—short *i*; yellow—long *o*; orange—short *o*; blue—long *u*; purple—short *u*.

2. Place a generous supply of markers, stickers, envelopes, and construction paper in the 10 colors in a spot convenient to the children.

Procedure

1. Ask children to read the key. Have each child choose a color and its corresponding vowel sound.

2. Have children select a sheet of paper in the color they chose and ask them to write at least 10 words with their vowel sound on the paper. They may decorate their papers with stickers and drawings.

3. Ask children to cut their papers into a few pieces to make puzzles. Have them place each puzzle in its own envelope.

4. Invite children to exchange envelopes with a partner, assemble the puzzles, and read the words on the puzzles aloud.

5. Have children return the puzzles to the envelopes. Save the puzzles to use again.

Switcheroo

Materials

- heavy construction
  paper or card stock
  in two colors
- scissors
- ruler
- markers
- writing paper
- pencils

Children make movable devices that let them change vowels in letter groups to make words.

Preparation

1. Cut one color of construction paper or card stock into 3-by-6-inch rectangles. You will need one rectangle for each child.

2. Cut paper or stock of a different color into strips about 1 by 8 inches. Make one strip for each child.

3. Turn each rectangle so that the longer side is horizontal. Cut a 1-inch horizontal slit in the center of each rectangle about an inch from the top. Cut a second slit about an inch from the bottom.

> *** Helpful Hint:** If you laminate the paper before you cut it, and then use permanent marker to write the letters, it will make the Switcheroos last longer and make sliding the letter strips easier.

Procedure

1. Give a rectangle and a strip to each child.

2. Ask children to place the strip in front of them and align it so the long side is vertical. Have children start at the top, leave at least an inch of space, and write a large letter a.

3. Have children continue to move down the strip writing the remaining vowels—e, i, o, u—under each other. Ask them to leave a bit of space between each letter and a blank inch at the bottom of the strip.

4. Next, have children place the rectangle in front of them so that the long side is horizontal. Tell them

they are going to write a letter or two to the left of the cut on the left and a letter or two to the right of the cut on the right. Have each child write different letter combinations. You may want to assign certain combinations or post a list of choices to reinforce what children have been studying. Here are some recommended letter combinations:

b-d, b-g, b-t, c-p, c-t, d-g, d-d, f-n, h-m, h-t, l-g, m-t, n-t, p-n, r-t, s-t, t-p, t-n, b-nd, l-ck, l-st, m-st, p-st, t-ck, w-ll, b-ke, c-ve, l-ne, m-le, p-le, r-ce, r-le, t-le, w-de

5. Ask children to hold the top of their vowel strip, pull it up carefully through the bottom slit on the rectangle, and then push it through the top slit until a vowel appears. Children can use the ends as tabs as they move the vowel strip to avoid pulling the strip all the way out of the rectangle.

6. Have children move the strips up and down and try to make a word with each vowel. They should list the words they make on sheets of paper.

7. After a few minutes, have children exchange Switcheroos and make more words. Continue for several more rounds. Save the Switcheroos to use again.

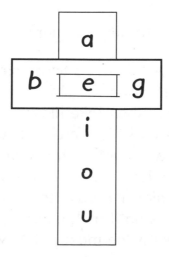

Scramble!

Materials

letter tiles
5-by-8-inch index cards
scissors
markers

This action game lets children practice making words with various long and short vowel sounds.

Preparation

1. You can make letter tiles by cutting index cards into small squares and writing a letter on each. Write several sets of alphabet letters, plus extra vowels.

2. To prepare the Scramble! cards, cut index cards in half. On each half, write clues that review vowel sounds and spelling, such as:

   - a short *a* word that ends with a *t*
   - any word that has long *o*
   - a long *u* sound word that doesn't have the letter *u*
   - a short *a* word that begins with *p*
   - a long *a* word that ends with *y*

Procedure

1. Divide the class into small groups. Give each group an equal number of letter tiles and of Scramble! cards.

2. Have each group sit in a circle. Ask children to spread their tiles faceup and stack their Scramble! cards facedown.

3. Instruct groups to play the game as follows:

   - The first player draws a Scramble! card and reads the clue on it aloud.
   - All the players then take tiles as needed and try to spell a word that fits the clue. The first player to do so gets two points. Others who do so get one point. All the letter tiles are returned to the pool.
   - The second player reads the next clue card.
   - Play continues until all the cards have been read. The player with the most points wins.

Word Burgers

Children make giant paper burgers and use words that have *r*-controlled vowels to label the parts.

Preparation

Create a sample word burger. Cut wide layers representing the burger, the other fillings, and the bun from construction paper. Write a word with an *r*-controlled vowel on each layer. You can use the word list at the back of this book for ideas. Glue the layers to the drawing paper to make a multilayered burger.

Materials

red, green, yellow, brown, and tan construction paper
scissors
colored pencils, crayons, or markers
glue
drawing paper

Procedure

1. Ask children to describe a hamburger they might order in a restaurant. What parts are essential? What do they like to have on their burgers? Explain to the children that today they are going to make word burgers.

2. Show the sample word burger to the class. Talk about the different layers and what they might represent (red—tomato slices or ketchup; green—pickles or lettuce; yellow—cheese or mustard; and so on).

3. Have children make the layers of the burgers from the colored paper. On each layer they should write a word that has an *r*-controlled vowel. (You can give *word burger* as an example of two words with *r*-controlled vowels.) You may wish to place a list of words with *r*-controlled vowels on the board.

4. Have children assemble their word burgers by gluing the parts to a piece of drawing paper. Ask children to read the words on their word burgers aloud to the class.

5. Display the word burgers in the classroom.

Double Combos

writing paper
pencils
books and magazines

Children sort two-syllable words by the vowel sounds in their syllables.

Procedure

1. Show children how to fold their papers into thirds and turn the papers so that the folds make vertical columns.

2. Have children label the first column *Double Long,* the second column *Double Short,* and the third column *Long and Short Combo.*

3. Write the word *syllable* on the board. Read it aloud and tell children that a syllable is a word or word part with a single vowel sound (for example, *cat* or *coat*). Explain how to tell if a word has two syllables. Give some examples of two-syllable words. Tell children that this activity will require children to think of two-syllable words that fit into the categories on their paper.

4. Ask the class to think of a two-syllable word that has a long vowel sound in both syllables. Have children write this word in the *Double Long* column. Have children suggest words that fit in the other two columns. You can refer to the lists below for examples in each category.

5. List the following words on the board in random order and ask children to write them in the proper categories on their papers:

   Double Long: baby, believe, cozy, daily, highway, lazy, maybe, rainbow, sailboat, shiny, silo, sleepy, snowflake, tasty, tightly

Double Short: asking, basket, cabin, children, foxes, happen, magic, packet, picnic, rabbit, rocket, sudden, trumpet, witches

Long and Short Combo: candy, inside, invite, island, frighten, mailbox, many, painting, penny, secret, snowman, study, sunny

6. Ask children to work on their own or in pairs to write two-syllable words in the columns. When they are done with the words you list, encourage them to search in books and magazines for words. If you like, you can award a small prize to the child or pair that finds the most words.

Wanted: Rule Breakers

Children issue warrants for words that break phonics rules and post their warrants on a wanted poster.

Materials

poster board
marker
brown shoe polish
cloth or paper towel
large envelope
glue
photocopies of page 43
scissors

Preparation

1. Tear or bend the edges of the poster board to make the wanted poster look beat-up. Use the marker to write *WANTED: Rule Breakers*. Rub shoe polish over the poster and wipe it off for an antique finish.

2. Cut the top from the envelope to create a pocket about 6 inches deep and glue the pocket to the poster. Hang the wanted poster in the classroom.

3. Make enough copies of page 43 so that each child can have several warrants. Cut each copy in half.

Procedure

1. Review some of the phonics rules that children have encountered in class. These may include rules like *Silent e at the end of a word gives the word's vowel the long sound,* or *When two vowels go walking, the first does the talking.* List several phonics rules on the board.

2. Explain that children will make out warrants for words that do not follow phonics rules. For example: *done* breaks the silent *e* rule, because it has a silent *e* but no long vowel sound. *Great* breaks the *first vowel does the talking* rule, because it is pronounced *grayt,* not *greet.*

3. Take a warrant and write *great* on the line next to *WANTED.* In the space below, write the phonics rule that *great* breaks. Place the warrant in the envelope on the poster.

4. Pass out warrants to each child. Encourage children to fill out warrants and place them in the envelope on the poster when they find rule-breaking words.

WANTED _____

RULE BREAKER

If it followed the rules,
it would say _____.
Instead it says _____.

WANTED _____

RULE BREAKER

If it followed the rules,
it would say _____.
Instead it says _____.

Hanging Around

Children discriminate between long and short vowel sounds to hang cutout "clothing" on the proper clothesline.

Preparation

1. Cut miniature clothing—simple shirts, skirts, pants, dresses, and socks—from the material or wallpaper samples. Use a marker to write a word with a long or a short vowel sound on each piece of clothing. (You may need to use a permanent marker to write on some materials.)

2. Place about the same amount of clothing in each basket, in no particular order.

3. String two clotheslines near each other, perhaps between the legs of two tables, attached to perpendicular walls in a corner, or on a bulletin board. Label two pieces of cloth or paper *Long* and *Short*. Attach one label to the middle of each clothesline with clothespins.

4. Place a few baskets of clothespins by the clotheslines.

Procedure

1. Divide the class into as many groups as you have baskets of clothing. Give each group a basket.

2. Show the clotheslines to the children and have them read the labels. Tell children they are going to sort the clothing and hang it on the lines.

3. Show children how to use a clothespin safely. Ask a volunteer to choose a piece of clothing from one of the baskets, read the word, and identify whether it

has a long or a short vowel sound. Then have the child use a clothespin to hang the piece of clothing on the long or short vowel line.

4. Let children take turns. They should continue hanging clothing until all the clothes are on the lines.

String Boards

Children use reusable manipulatives to practice identifying vowel sounds and reading words.

Materials

cardboard, foam board, or heavy poster board
marker
ruler
scissors or paper cutter
glue
duct tape (optional)
yarn of two different colors
magazine illustrations, clip art, stickers, or stamps and ink pad
masking tape

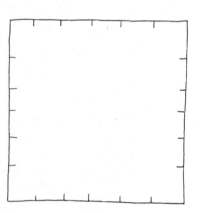

Preparation

String boards can take many forms and can be used in many different ways. Choose whether you want to use string boards for all the vowel sounds or just certain ones. Make large string boards to practice all the vowel sounds or use smaller ones to tackle one vowel at a time.

1. Select a large square of cardboard, foam board, or poster board. Use the ruler and a marker to make inch-long parallel lines all around the perimeter, perpendicular to the perimeter. Make 20 lines, spaced evenly around the board. Use sharp scissors or a paper cutter to cut slits along the lines.

2. Measure from the center of the board to the corner. Add 4 inches to this measurement. Cut 10 strands of yarn this length in one color and 10 strands in a second color.

3. Near the top of the board, in the center, use a large piece of masking tape to attach five strands of one color of yarn radiating to the left and five strands of a different color radiating to the right. Label the two pieces of tape with two different vowel sounds; for instance, *Long* e and *Short* e.

4. Follow the same procedure with the remaining yarn for the lower half of the board. Keep the vowel labels the same; if you labeled the top cluster of red yarn *Long* e, give the lower cluster of red yarn the same label.

5. Next to each slit around the edge, glue a small picture of an object or write a word that contains one of the vowel sounds with which you have labeled the board. You can draw the pictures or use magazine photos, clip art, stickers, or stamped images.

Procedure

1. Ask children to read the names of the vowel sounds listed in the center of the board. Explain that their task is to look at a picture on the board and use the yarn to connect the proper vowel sound to the slit next to the picture.

2. Have a volunteer choose a picture, say the name aloud, and identify the vowel sound. Then direct him or her to insert the free end of a strand of yarn into the slit next to the picture so that the vowel sound correlates. For example, if the picture is of an egg, the child should attach a strand of the yarn to the slit by the picture from the cluster labeled *Short e*.

3. Have children continue until all 20 pieces of yarn have been attached.

4. Children can check one another's answers.

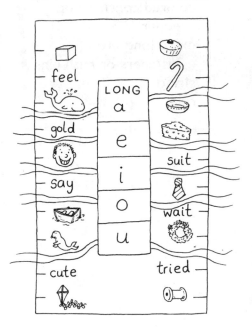

Balloon Match

Children use a colorful poster to match words and their vowel sounds.

Preparation

1. Seal the envelopes shut and cut them in half crosswise to make deep pockets. Glue these 10 pockets to the right side of the foam board or poster board.

2. Cut 10 balloon shapes from the colored construction paper. Write a different long or short vowel sound on each shape; for example, *Long i* or *Short u*. Glue the shapes, one below the other, to the left side of the board.

3. Attach a brad fastener to the base of each balloon and to the left of each envelope pocket. Make sure that a loop of string will fit easily over each brad.

4. Measure the diagonal length of the board. Cut 10 pieces of string this length. Tie one end of each piece of string securely to the brad attached to each balloon. Tie a loop in the other end of the string large enough to go over the head of another brad.

5. Write the words children will study at the top of index cards, so that they will be visible when the cards are placed sticking up in the pockets. You can use the word list at the back of this book. Make several packs of word cards, with 10 cards in each pack. In each pack, include one word for each of the 10 long and short vowel sounds.

Instead of using foam board or poster board, Balloon Match can be a bulletin board display. As such, you may need to adapt the design by placing the balloons across the top of the bulletin board and the envelope pockets along the bottom so that children can reach them. Make sure the strings are long enough to reach from the upper right balloon to the lower left pocket. Use push pins instead of brads to connect the strings.

Procedure

1. Place a deck of 10 word cards in front of a small group of children. Read the words together. Then ask a volunteer to read a word and place the word card in an empty pocket. Continue until all the cards have been placed in pockets.

2. Ask a volunteer to reread the word in the first pocket and identify the corresponding vowel sound balloon. Have the child take the string from the balloon and attach the loop at the free end to the brad next to the matching word.

3. Continue in this manner until all the words and balloons have been matched. Then remove the strings and the word cards. Try the activity again with a different pack of word cards.

4. You can make the activity self-checking. Use 10 different colors for the balloons. Mark a small matching color dot on the back of each word card. Once children match a balloon to a word, they can turn the card over to see if the colors match.

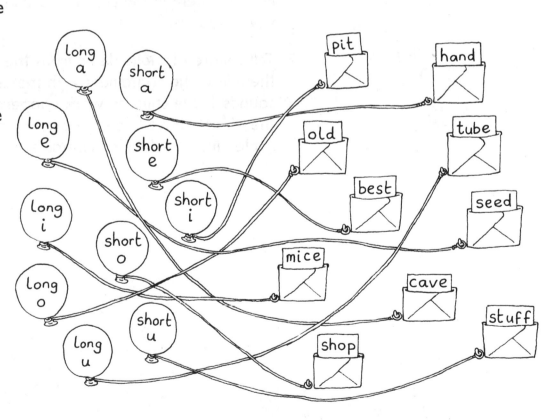

Sort It Out

large basket
marker
items or pictures to
   represent long or
   short vowel sounds:
   tie, rope, top, lid, cup,
   brush, comb, stick,
   sock, ring, cane, and
   so on
containers to represent
   long or short vowel
   sounds: can, mitt,
   bowl, pot, box, dish,
   tub, tube, and so on

Children sort objects that represent various long and short vowel sounds.

Preparation

1. Place all the items or pictures in a large basket. Label the basket *To be sorted.*

2. Label each of the containers with the vowel sound it represents. For example, the can would be labeled *Short a,* and the pot *Short o.* Make sure the items can fit in the containers. If this is problematic, use pictures of items instead.

Procedure

1. This activity is most effective with groups of four or five children. Show the containers to the group. Have children identify the containers and then read the vowel sounds.

2. Tell children to take items from the box and sort them into the containers with matching vowel sounds. Have children work cooperatively until all the objects have been removed from the box and sorted into the labeled containers.

Skits

The skits that follow will help you teach vowel sound concepts to your students in an engaging and entertaining fashion. The skits call for simple letter costumes, and some ask for props. You will also need word cards, which can be made from construction paper or poster board, for several of the skits.

You can make simple letter costumes by cutting poster board into squares. Punch two holes at the top of each square, loop a piece of yarn from one hole to the other, and tie it. Label each square with the letter called for in the skit. Hang the letter squares around children's necks. You can also cut large letters out of colorful felt and attach them to children's clothing with safety pins. Or you can write the letters on old T-shirts.

If you don't have some of the required props on hand, substitute magazine illustrations. You may want to mount the cutout illustrations on poster board to make them more durable.

Children will need varying amounts of help to read and understand the skits. You can use your judgment about helping children to read and practice saying the dialogue. They do not need to memorize their lines; they can simply hold the script in one hand while performing. If a role requires that an actor hold props, you may want to have a table nearby on which scripts can be placed.

For each skit, there is a worksheet that reinforces the concept dramatized in the skit. After each performance, ask children to complete the corresponding worksheet. You will find the skit worksheets at the end of the Reproducible Worksheets section, starting on page 69.

When Two Vowels Go Walking

Concept

In most one-syllable words with pairs of vowels, the first vowel is pronounced and the second vowel is silent.

Introduction

- Tell the class that the title of this skit is When Two Vowels Go Walking. Explain that the complete rule is: *When two vowels go walking, the first does the talking.*

Write the word *team* on the board. Ask the class to identify the vowels in *team*. Ask, *Which vowel comes first? When you say the word* team, *do you hear the* e *say its own name? It is doing the talking for the two vowels. The* a *does not make a sound. It stays silent.*

Write the word *coat* on the board. Ask the class, *Which two vowels are walking in this word? Which one will do the talking?* Say *coat*. Ask, *Do you hear the* o *say its own name?*

PRODUCTION NOTES

Cast
10 cast members, each wearing a square with the letter A, B, D, E, I, M, N, O, R, or T.

Stage Directions
B and T, M and N, and R and D are pairs. The actors in each pair stand facing the audience, with the first in each pair stage right and the other about four feet to the left.

When Two Vowels Go Walking

Consonants stand in their places as **O** *and* **A** *enter.* **O** *is holding* **A's** *right hand.*

A: What do you want to do?

O: We are going to make some words.

You won't have to say a thing.

I will do all the talking.

When two vowels go walking, the first does the talking.

O *and* **A** *walk between* **B** *and* **T**. **A** *puts a hand over its mouth.*

O: Boat.

O *and* **A** *walk between* **M** *and* **N**.

O: Moan.

O *and* **A** *walk between* **R** *and* **D**.

O: Road.

Both vowels move away, and **O** *walks off the stage.*

E *enters and takes* **A's** *right hand.*

A: What do you want to do?

E: I want to make some words.

You won't have to say a thing.

I will do all the talking.

When two vowels go walking, the first does the talking.

*The vowel pair moves between **B** and **T**.*

E: Beat.

***E** and **A** walk between **M** and **N**.*

E: Mean.

***E** and **A** walk between **R** and **D**.*

E: Read.

*Both vowels move away, and **E** walks off the stage.*

***I** enters and takes **A's** right hand.*

A: Do you want to make some words?

I: I will go with you. But I am too tired to do any work.

A: Don't worry, I'll be first. You won't have to say a thing.

When two vowels go walking, the first does the talking.

***I** puts a hand over its mouth.*

The vowel pair moves between each consonant pair in turn.

A: Bait.

A: Main.

A: Raid.

*Both vowels move away. **A** walks off the stage.*

*The consonants move away, except for **T** and **D**.*

These consonants stand apart, not in a pair.

***I** and **E** step forward.*

I: Would you like to make some words?

E (whispering): Yes, but my throat is getting sore.

    I don't want to say much.

I: Don't worry, I will go first. You won't have to say a thing.

    When two vowels go walking, the first does the talking.

*This time **I** takes **E's** right hand. **E** covers its mouth.*

*The vowels move over to stand first next to **D**, and then next to **T**.*

I: Tie.

I: Die.

All the vowels come on stage as the consonants leave.

All Vowels: When two vowels go walking, the first does

    the talking.

The Sale

Concept

In a one-syllable word with CVC silent *e*, the first vowel is long.

Introduction

Write *man, rid, not,* and *cub* on the board. Have a volunteer read the words. Ask the class what type of vowel sound, long or short, they hear in each word. Then have the children close their eyes. Add *e* to the end of each word. Ask a volunteer to read the new words. Have the class identify the type of sound in each word. Say, *The silent* e *at the end of the word makes the first vowel say its own name. This makes the vowel have a long sound.*

Write *pal, dim,* and *rod* on the board. Read the words together. Ask the class what type of vowel sound they hear in each word. Have a volunteer change the first word to one with a long vowel sound. Have another volunteer read the new word. Do the same for the other two words.

Say, *Today's skit is about a salesperson. The salesperson wants to sell lots of words to make everyone happy. Let's see what the salesperson does to sell words.*

PRODUCTION NOTES

Props
table or desk
play money
three one-word cards: *can/kit/hop* (Leave space on each card to write the letter *e*.)

Cast
Salesperson, Customer One, Customer Two, Customer Three

Stage Directions
Put the word cards on the table. Provide a marker for the Salesperson. Give some play money to each of the Customers.

The Sale

• •

Salesperson enters and stands behind the table. **Customers** *enter and stand to one side.*

Salesperson: Oh dear, I do not have many words left to sell.

I hope people will want to buy what I have.

Calls out loudly: Words for sale! Words! Words for sale!

Customer One (*walking up to* **Salesperson**): Do you have any words with the long *a* vowel sound?

Salesperson: I have **can**.

Customer One: I don't want **can**. That has the short *a* sound.

Begins to walk away.

Salesperson: Wait! I can fix it for you. *Writes the letter e at the end of the word.*
Look, this silent *e* makes the first vowel say its name. Now the word is **cane**. **Cane** has the long *a* sound.

Customer One: I'll take it. *Pays and exits.*

Customer Two (*walking up to* **Salesperson**): Do you have any words with the long *i* sound?

Salesperson: I have **kit**. Would you like to buy **kit**?

Customer Two: **Kit** has the short *i* sound. I do not want it.

Salesperson: I can fix it up for you. *Writes the letter e at the end of the word.* This silent e will make the *i* say its name. Now it has the long vowel sound. It says **kite**.

Customer Two: Oh, I love kites! I will buy the word.

Pays and exits.

Salesperson: I only have one word left. I hope someone wants to buy it.

Customer Three (*walking up to* **Salesperson**): I need to buy a word with the long *o* sound. You only have one word left. Does it have the long *o* sound?

Salesperson: I have the word **hop**. That has the short *o* sound. But I can change **hop** for you. *Writes e at the end of* **hop**.

This is a silent e. It makes the first vowel say its name. Now the word is **hope**. The word **hope** has the long *o* sound.

Customer Three: That is just what I need! I'll take it.

Pays and exits.

Salesperson (*waving all the money in the air*): I like to make people happy, and I really like to sell words!

The Sad Letter R

Concept

When a vowel is followed by *r*, the *r* changes the sound of the vowel. These sounds are called *r*-controlled vowels.

Introduction

Write the following words on the board: *tan, pail,* and *star.* Say to the class, *Read the first word. Who can tell me the vowel sound in this word? Look at the second word. What vowel sound do we hear? Now look at the word* star. *It has a vowel sound that is neither short nor long. The* r *changes the way we say the vowel. Say* star.

Write these words on the board: *fern, stir, sport,* and *hurt.* Have children read each of these words. Say, *The letter* r *changes each of the vowels. When we read these words, we hear the* r *more than we hear a vowel.*

Say, *This skit is about the letter* r. *We will find out why the title is The Sad Letter* R.

PRODUCTION NOTES

Props
two one-word cards: *barn / wonderful*
seven two-word cards: *bun, burn / pat, part / he, her / cat, cart / bid, bird / cub, curb / hose, horse*
one four-word card: *party, soccer, park, roller-coaster*

Cast
R (wearing a square with the letter *R*), Friend, and Word Kid

Stage Directions
R and Friend are stage right. Word Kid stands at stage left and holds up the correct word card each time one of the words on the cards is spoken.

The Sad Letter R

• •

*R is sitting alone crying. **Friend** enters and walks toward **R**.*

Friend: Why are you crying?

R: No one wants to play with me. They think I am bossy.

Friend: Why do they think you are bossy?

R: I change the way a word sounds.

Look at the word **bun**.   With me it says **burn**.

The word **pat** changes to **part**, and **he** changes to **her**,

all because of me! I don't mean to be bossy.

But when I change the way a word sounds,

the meaning changes, too.

R starts crying again.

Friend: Please don't cry!

R: Even animals run away from me. I like animals!

Friend: Why do they run away?

R: I change the way their names sound and what they mean.

Look at the word **cat**. When I come along,

cat says **cart**. See, no more cat!

A **cub** changes to **curb** when I am around.

Then there is no more baby bear, just part of a street.

R begins crying again.

Friend: Don't be sad. I will show you some animals that need you.

Look at **bid**. With you, it can be **bird**. The word **hose** changes to **horse** when you come along. And even the horse needs you to make a **barn** for it.
You are really a very **wonderful** letter.

R (*smiling*)**:** That's true. Maybe I'm not so bad. Maybe I can have some fun.

Friend: We can play **together**. With your help we can go to a **party**. We can play **soccer** in the **park**. Maybe we can even go on a **roller coaster**.
Come on, let's go!

R and **Friend** *leave the stage smiling and laughing.*

A Trip with O and W

Concept

Two sounds can occur when *o* and *w* are paired in words. The first is the sound in *cow*. The second is the long *o* sound in *glow*.

Introduction

Write the words *slow* and *cow* on the board. Say to the class, *What two letters are the same in both of these words?* Circle *ow* in each. Read the words to the class. Ask, *What vowel sound do you hear in the first word?* (long o) *What vowel sound is in the second word? It is not long or short. It sounds like what you say when you are hurt —OW! When you see o and w together, you must try both sounds and then decide which one makes sense. This skit is about o and w. Listen carefully to hear the two sounds these letters make.*

PRODUCTION NOTES

Props

two chairs

steering wheel (a paper plate or Frisbee; optional)

10 one-word cards: *cow / brown / now / town / glow / know / rainbow / blow / snow / now*

one two-word card: *slow, down*

one three-word card: *window, clown, bow*

Cast

O, W, and Word Kid

Stage Directions

Word Kid holds up the correct word card each time one of the words on the cards is spoken.

A Trip with O and W

O and W are seated side by side, as if in a car; W is driving and O is sleeping; **Word Kid** stands at the side and holds up the correct word card each time one of the words on the cards is spoken.

W looks around and pokes O in the ribs.

O: OW!!

W: Look! I see a **cow**.

O: Yes, it is **brown**. *O goes back to sleep.*

W pokes O again.

O: OW!! What is it **now**?

W: Wake up. We're coming into **town**.

O: Then you'd better **slow down**.

W: Look out the **window**. I see a **clown** wearing a big red **bow**.

O: What is that **glow** up in the sky?

W: I don't **know**.

O: Ooooh, it's a pretty **rainbow**.

W: I think the wind is starting to **blow**. A storm is coming.

O: It might even **snow**!

W: I'll drive home **now**. Here we go.

Aw, It's So Cute!

Concept

The letter combination *aw* creates a unique sound.

Introduction

Write the following words on the board: *paw, claw, dawn, law, fawn, shawl.* Tell the class, *Look carefully at these words. Which two letters are the same in every word?* Circle *aw* in each word. *Let's read the words together. Which sound does* aw *make? When* a *and* w *are together, they make this special sound. The skit we are performing today uses lots of words with this sound. Listen carefully to hear the sound that* aw *makes.*

PRODUCTION NOTES

Props
three chairs
actual items, models, or pictures of the following: kitten, baby, landscape drawing, dinner of liver and spinach, flower, scarecrow
six one-word cards: *crawl / draw / yawn / awful / saw / straw*

Cast
A, W, Narrator

Stage Directions
Narrator, A, and W sit on chairs. A and W sit very close together, with A on the right. A holds up the appropriate prop or picture and names the item each time an *aw* word is spoken. Narrator holds up the word card for each *aw* word.

Aw, It's So Cute!

Narrator: Today we are talking with the letters **A** and **W**. They have brought some special things to show us. Listen to these, **A** and **W**. See whether you can hear the sound they make together.

A: A kitten.

W: Aw! How cute!

Narrator: Do you see the kitten **yawn**?

A: A baby.

W: Aw! How sweet!

Narrator: This little baby can **crawl**.

A: A picture.

W: Aw! That is very nice!

Narrator: Do you like to **draw**?

A: A dinner of liver and spinach.

W: Aw! That looks yucky!

Narrator: I think that dinner would be **awful**.

A: A flower.

W: Aw! That is very pretty!

Narrator: I think I **saw** a bee on the flower.

A: A scarecrow.

W: Aw, that doesn't scare me!

Narrator: A scarecrow is stuffed with **straw**.

A (*points to the narrator*)**:** A narrator.

W: Aw! Didn't our narrator do a good job?

Narrator: What sound do you hear when **a** and **w** come together? Say it with us.

All: Aw!!

Reproducible Worksheets

There are three types of worksheets in this section. The first are coloring pages. Children read the words on these pages and color the pictures according to their vowel sounds. Included are worksheets for the long and short sounds of single vowels, other long vowels, and combinations of long and short vowels. You can use these coloring sheets for review or to reteach or assess your students.

The second type of worksheet requires students to fill in vowels in words with blanks. Children read hints or clues to help them complete these words. They then fill in the correct vowels from lists of choices. You can use these worksheets to provide additional practice with long and short vowels. For each worksheet, you can also lead children in a writing activity that requires them to use the words in sentences.

At the end of this section are the worksheets designed to accompany the skits. There is one worksheet for each skit.

Coloring: Sounds of a

Color long *a* red. Color short *a* blue.

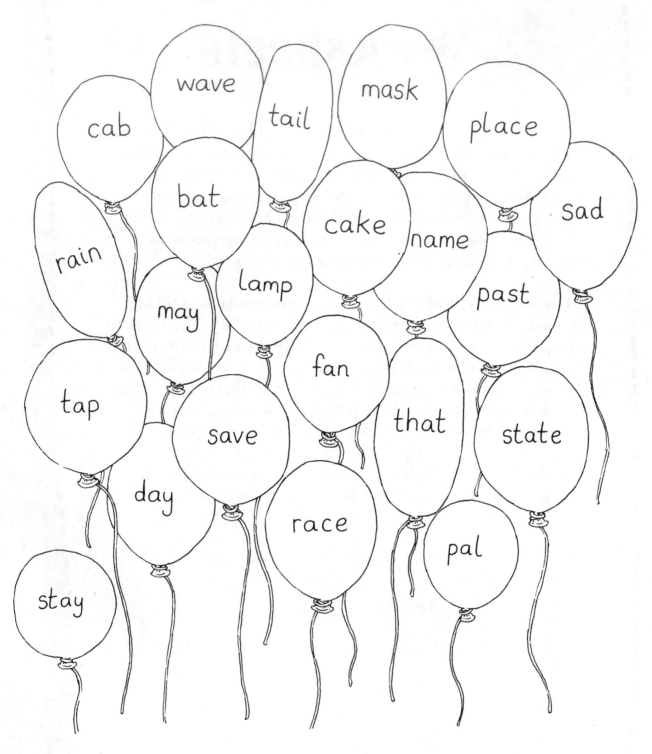

Coloring: Sounds of e

Color long e blue. Color short e yellow.

Name _____

Coloring: Sounds of *i*

Color long *i* orange. Color short *i* purple.

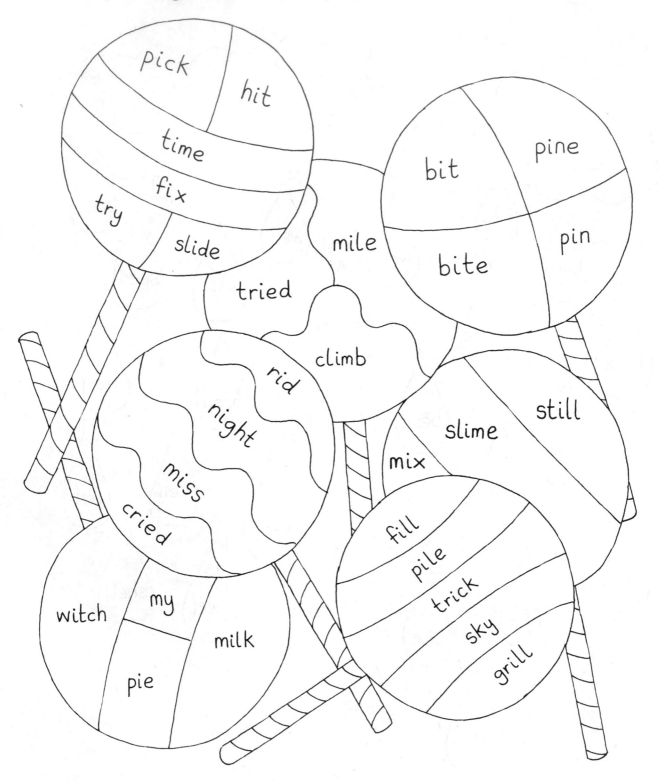

Coloring: Sounds of o

Color long o red. Color short o purple. Color the leaves green.

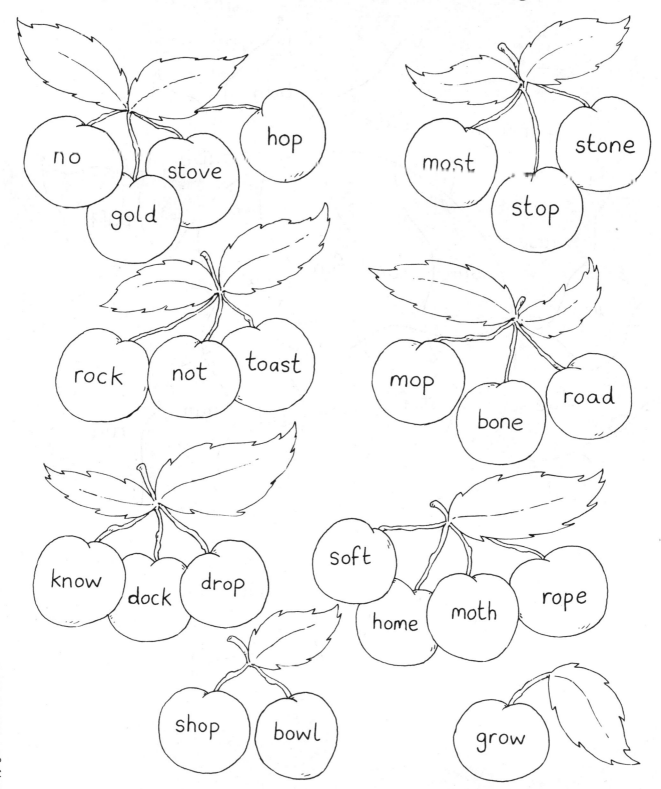

Coloring: Sounds of u

Color long *u* orange. Color short *u* yellow.

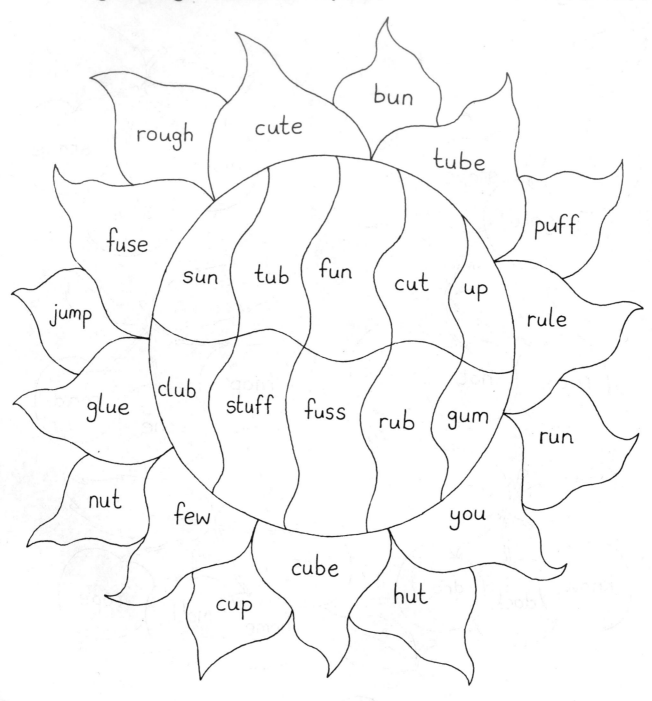

Coloring: Long Vowels

Color long *a* green. Color long *e* blue. Color long *i* red. Color long *o* purple. Color long *u* yellow.

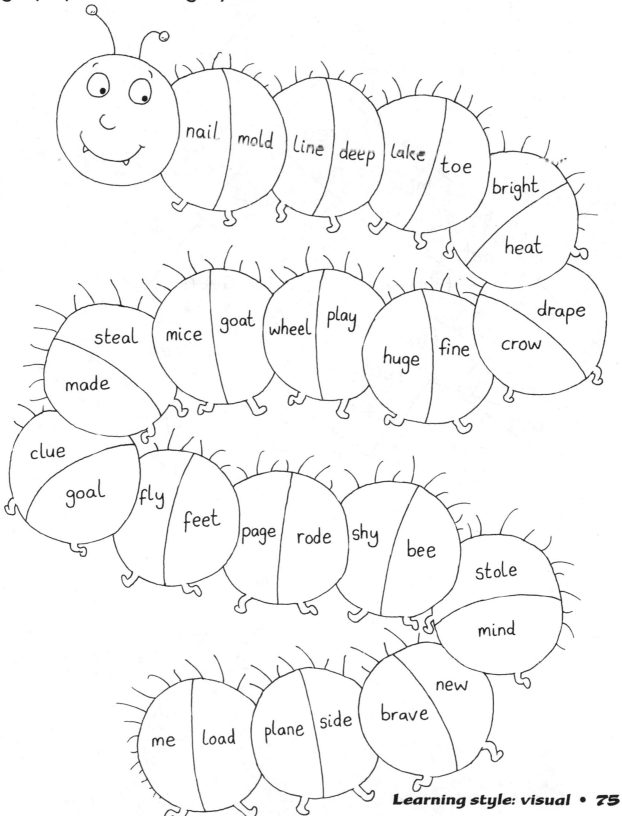

Name _____

Coloring: Mixed Vowel Sounds

Color long e green. Color short e red. Color long *i* blue. Color short *i* yellow. Color long *o* orange. Color short *o* purple.

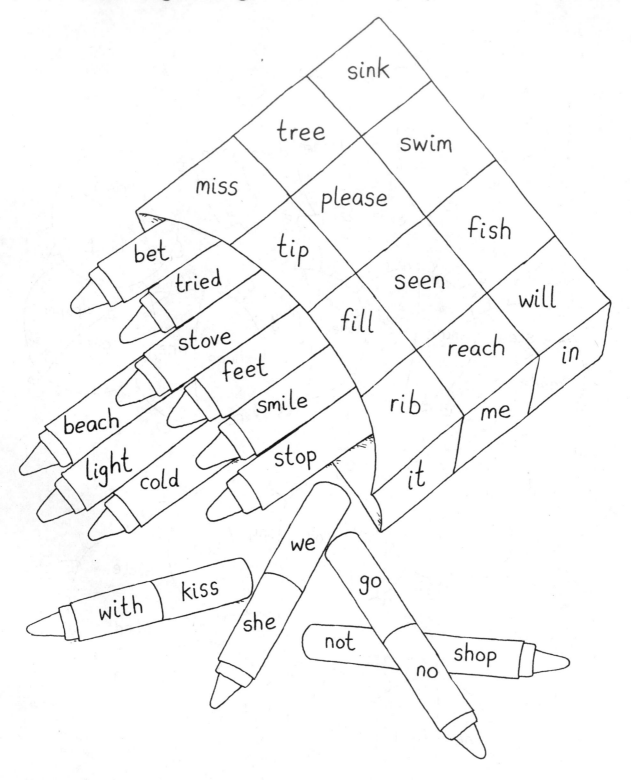

Coloring: Mixed Vowel Sounds

Color long *a* green. Color short *a* blue. Color long *e* purple. Color short *e* red. Color long *i* orange. Color short *i* yellow. Color long *o* pink. Color short *o* brown.

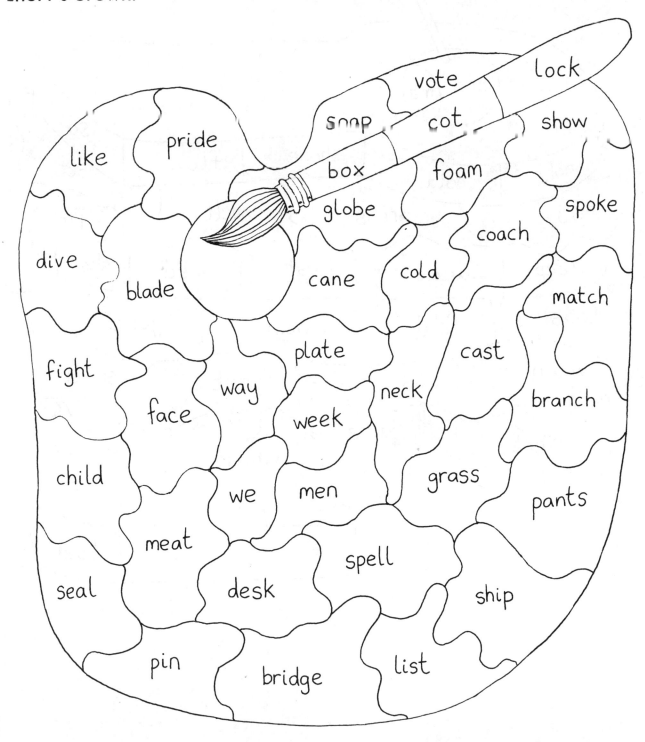

Coloring: Mixed Vowel Sounds

Color long e red. Color short *i* orange. Color short e green. Color long o brown. Color long *i* yellow.

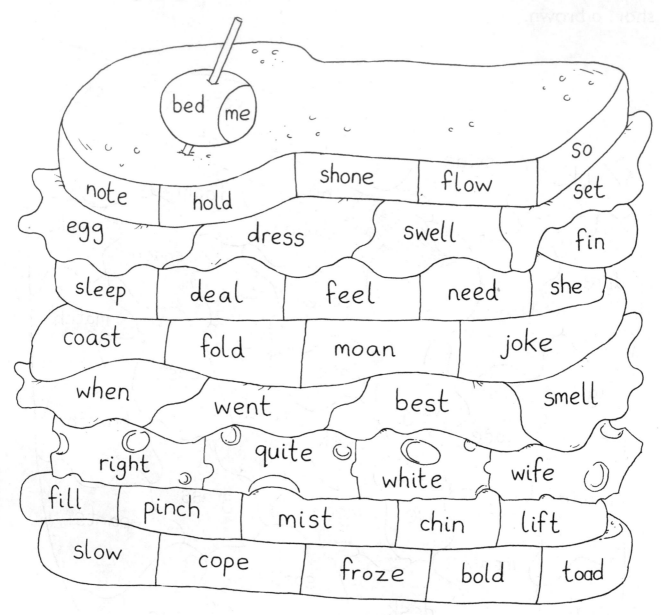

Coloring: Mixed Vowel Sounds

Color long *a* brown. Color short *a* yellow. Color long *i* red. Color long *u* pink. Color short *u* orange.

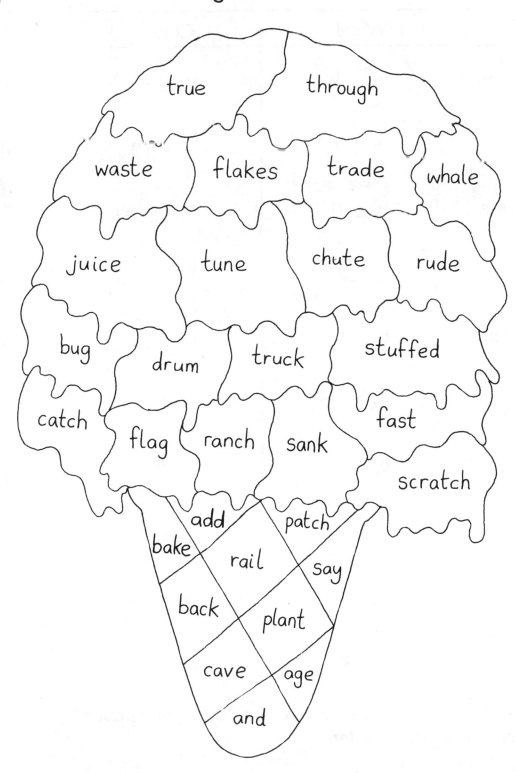

Name _____

Clues: Using a, e, or o

Read the clues. Write *a*, *e*, or *o* to spell a word that goes with each clue.

Clue	Word	Clue	Word
spider's home	w___b	angry	m___d
not dry	w___t	chicken	h___n
bird's home	n___st	a number	t___n
cry	s___b	tie	kn___t
for baseball	b___t	hat	c___p
fix	m___nd	kitten	c___t
pan	p___t	soda	p___p
happy	gl___d	corn	c___b
ask and ask	b___g	airplane	j___t
stone	r___ck	jump	h___p

Pick three of the words you wrote. Turn over your paper.
Write each word in a sentence.

Clues: Using e, i, or u

Read the clues. Write e, i, or u to spell a word that goes with each clue.

Clue	Word	Clue	Word
chew this	g___m	a color	r___d
hop	J___mp	pull	t___g
large	b___g	it rings	b___ll
slice	c___t	hole	p___t
cup	m___g	5 + 1	s___x
wet dirt	m___d	it writes	p___n
carpet	r___g	stick	tw___g
smile	gr___n	ant	b___g
fake hair	w___g	turtle's back	sh___ll
use money	sp___nd	water bird	d___ck

Pick three of the words you wrote. Turn over your paper.
Write as many words that rhyme with each word as you can.

Clues: Using *a* or *i*

Read the clues. Write *a* or *i* to spell a word that goes with each clue.

Clue	Word	Clue	Word
run	r___ce	big grin	sm___le
glue	p___ste	long walk	h___ke
stops cars	br___kes	stack	p___le
garden tool	r___ke	story	t___le
bold	br___ve	alike	s___me
cook in oven	b___ke	two times	tw___ce
bat home	c___ve	fruit	gr___pe
ten cents	d___me	snow	fl___kes
3 + 6	n___ne	two-wheelers	b___kes
fire	fl___me	kind of tree	p___ne

Pick six of the words you wrote. Turn over your paper.
Use the six words in a poem or a story.

Name _____

Clues: Using o or u

Read the clues. Write *o* or *u* to spell a word that goes with each clue.

Clue	Word	Clue	Word
dog treat	b___ne	toothpaste	t___be
sleep	d___ze	law	r___le
ice cream	c___ne	not polite	r___de
an animal	m___le	funny riddle	j___ke
wish	h___pe	very big	h___ge
sand hill	d___ne	house	h___me
flag holder	p___le	song	t___ne
world map	gl___be	month	J___ne
kind of flower	r___se	rock	st___ne
not cut	wh___le	box	c___be

Pick five of the words you wrote. Turn over your paper.
Write as many rhyming words as you can for each word.

Name _____

Clues: Using *ai* or *oa*

Read the clues. Write *ai* or *oa* to spell a word that goes with each clue.

Clue	Word	Clue	Word
bucket	p____l	ship	b____t
street	r____d	wash with	s____p
mind	br____n	letters	m____l
jacket	c____t	prison	j____l
moan	gr____n	fish food	b____t
hike this	tr____l	gave money	p____d
front of neck	thr____t	frog	t____d
spot	st____n	hammer this	n____l
runs on tracks	tr____n	bread	l____f
bubbles	f____m	dogs wag this	t____l

Pick five of the words you wrote. Turn over your paper. Draw a picture for each word. Write a sentence that tells about the picture.

84 • *Learning style: visual*

Name _____

Clues: Using *ea* or *ie*

Read the clues. Write *ea* or *ie* to spell a word that goes with each clue.

Clue	Word	Clue	Word
cooked in oil	fr____d	seashore	b____ch
monster	h____st	not dirty	cl____n
hit a drum	b____t	used a towel	dr____d
low cost	ch____p	make hot	h____t
sobbed	cr____d	lots of food	f____st
blue pants	j____ns	get better	h____l
a fruit	p____ch	did your best	tr____d
lunch or dinner	m____l	fibbed	l____d
chair	s____t	water animal	s____l
knotted	t____d	not strong	w____k

Pick five of the words you wrote. Turn over your paper.
Write each word in a sentence.

When Two Vowels Go Walking: Identifying Long *a, e, i,* and *o*

Circle the first vowel in each word. Read the words. Each vowel with a circle says its name.

loan	pail	meal	cried
coat	team	boat	mail
tried	moan	dream	lied
rain	paid	beat	road

Write each word in the correct box.

long a	**long e**	**long i**	**long o**

The Sale: Making Vowels Long with Silent e

Read the words below. Then add the letter e to the end of each of the words. Read the new words. Draw a line from each word to the matching picture.

1. can___

2. kit___

3. pin___

4. cub___

5. man___

6. rob___

7. tub___

8. dim___

Name _____

The Sad Letter R: Unscrambling Words

Look at each picture. Unscramble the letters to make the word. Write the word on the line.

1. m r a  _____

2. r b n a _____

3. t s a r  _____

4. a c r _____

5. r i d b  _____

6. o r n c  _____

7. r c h a  _____

8. a d c r _____

9. r k o f _____

10. l r t t e u  _____

11. r j a _____

12. k a s r h  _____

88 • *Learning style: visual*

A Trip with O and W: Identifying *ow* Sounds

Read each sentence. Look at the underlined word. If *ow* makes the long *o* sound, use a yellow crayon to circle the word. If *ow* makes the sound in *cow*, use a brown crayon.

1. I see a <u>cow</u>.

2. It is <u>brown</u>.

3. We are coming into <u>town</u>.

4. You'd better <u>slow</u> <u>down</u>.

5. Look out the <u>window</u>.

6. I see a <u>clown</u> wearing a big, red <u>bow</u>.

7. What is that <u>glow</u> up in the sky?

8. I don't <u>know</u>.

9. It is a pretty <u>rainbow</u>.

10. I think the wind is starting to <u>blow</u>.

11. It might even <u>snow</u>!

12. I will drive us home <u>now</u>.

Aw, It's So Cute!: Identifying *aw* Sounds

For each sentence, fill in the blank with a word from the Word Bank that makes sense.

crawl	dawn	draw	law
saw	straw	thaw	yawn

1. The sun comes up at _____.

2. When I am sleepy, I _____.

3. A scarecrow is filled with _____.

4. That bug may _____ up my leg!

5. You need a _____ to cut the wood.

6. The hot sun will _____ the ice.

7. Please _____a picture for me.

8. A rule may also be a _____.

WORD LIST

Short a
add
and
ant
ask
back
bag
band
bank
bat
bath
black
branch
cab
calf
cap
cast
cat
catch
class
crab
crack
crash
dad
damp
fan
fast
fat
flag
flat
gap
gas
glass
grass

half
ham
hand
hat
jam
lamp
land
last
mad
man
mask
match
pack
pad
pal
pants
pass
past
pat
patch
plan
plants
quack
rack
rag
raft
ramp
ranch
rat
sack
sad
sang
sank
scab

scratch
splash
stack
stamp
stand
tag
tan
tank
tap
task
track
trap
trash
van
wag

Short e
bed
beg
bell
belt
bench
bend
best
bet
cent
check
chef
chest
desk
dress
egg
elf
end

felt
hem
hen
jet
kept
left
leg
let
melt
men
mess
met
neck
nest
net
pen
pest
pet
press
red
rent
rest
sent
set
shelf
shell
sled
smell
spell
spent
stem
step
stretch
swell

tell
ten
tent
test
them
then
twelve
vent
vest
web
well
went
west
wet
when

Short i
bib
bit
brick
bridge
chill
chin
clip
crib
dig
dill
dip
dish
ditch
drill
drink
fill
fin

fish	ring	box	rob	dust
fist	rink	chop	rock	fudge
fix	rip	clock	rod	fun
flip	ship	cob	rot	fuss
grill	sift	cot	shock	gull
grin	sing	crop	shop	gum
grip	sink	dock	shot	hug
hit	sit	dog	sob	hunt
in	spit	dot	sock	hut
inch	split	drop	sod	judge
ink	spring	flock	soft	jug
inn	stick	flop	spot	jump
it	still	fox	stop	just
itch	sting	frog	top	luck
kick	string	got	trot	lump
king	swim	hog		mud
kiss	swing	hop	**Short u**	mug
knit	switch	hot	brush	must
lick	thin	job	bud	nut
lift	tip	jog	bug	plug
list	trick	knob	bump	plum
milk	trim	knock	bun	puff
mint	trip	knot	bunch	punch
miss	twig	lock	bus	pup
mist	twins	lodge	but	rub
mitt	whip	log	club	rug
mix	wig	lot	crumb	run
pick	will	mob	crunch	rust
pig	win	mop	crush	scrub
pin	wink	moth	crust	shrub
pinch	witch	not	cub	shrug
pink	with	odd	cuff	shut
pit	wish	off	cup	stub
pitch		plot	cut	stuff
rib	**Short o**	pod	drum	stump
rich	block	pond	duck	such
rid	blond	pot	dump	sun

92 • **Word List**

thumb
truck
trust
tub
tug
up
us

Long a

age
aim
bait
bake
base
bay
blade
braid
brain
brake
brave
cage
cake
came
cane
case
cave
chain
claim
clay
crane
date
day
drain
drape
face
fade
fake

fail
faith
flake
flame
frame
gain
game
gate
grain
grape
gray
hail
hate
hay
jail
lace
laid
lake
lame
late
lay
made
maid
mail
make
mane
may
nail
name
page
paid
pail
pain
paint
pale
pay
place

plane
plate
play
pray
race
raid
rail
rain
raise
rake
rate
ray
sail
sale
same
save
say
scale
scrape
shade
shave
skate
snail
snake
space
sprain
spray
stage
stain
state
stay
strain
stray
tail
tale
tame
tape

trade
trail
train
tray
vase
wail
wait
wake
waste
wave
way
whale

Long e

be
beach
bead
beak
beam
bean
beast
beat
bee
beef
beet
bleach
bleed
cheap
cheat
cheek
cheese
clean
creak
cream
crease
creek
deal

deep
dream
east
eat
eve
feast
feed
feel
feet
flea
freak
free
freeze
geese
grease
greed
green
greet
he
heal
heap
heat
heel
jeans
jeep
keep
knee
kneel
leak
leap
me
meal
meat
meet
neat
need
pea

peach	three	high	shy	**Long o**
peek	treat	hike	side	blow
please	tree	ice	sigh	boast
reach	we	kind	sight	boat
real	weak	kite	sign	bold
reel	weed	knife	sky	bone
queen	week	knight	slice	bowl
scene	wheat	lie	slide	broke
scream	wheel	lied	slime	choke
screen	wreath	light	smile	close
seal		like	spice	coach
seat	**Long i**	lime	spy	coal
see	bike	line	strike	coast
seed	bite	mice	style	coat
seen	bride	might	tide	cold
sheet	bright	mild	tie	colt
sleep	by	mile	tied	cone
sleeve	child	mind	tight	cope
sneak	climb	mine	tile	crow
sneeze	cried	my	time	doe
speak	cry	nice	tribe	dome
speed	dice	night	tried	doze
squeak	die	nine	try	drove
squeeze	died	pie	twice	float
steal	dime	pile	type	flow
steam	dive	pine	vine	foam
streak	dry	pipe	white	fold
stream	eye	pride	why	froze
street	fight	prize	wide	globe
sweep	file	pry	wife	glow
sweet	fine	quite	wild	go
tea	fire	rhyme	wine	goal
teach	flight	rice	wipe	goat
team	fly	right	wise	goes
teeth	fried	ripe	write	gold
theme	fry	rise		groan
these	hide	shine		grow

hoe	shone	crew	**R-Controlled Vowels**	***ar* as in *air***
hold	show	crude		bare
hole	slope	cube		blare
home	slow	cute	***ar* as in *arc***	care
hope	smoke	dew	arch	dare
hose	so	drew	are	fare
joke	soak	dune	arm	flare
know	soap	few	art	glare
low	sold	flew	bar	hare
load	sole	flute	bark	pare
loaf	spoke	fume	barn	rare
loan	stole	fuse	car	scarce
moan	stone	glue	card	scare
mold	stove	grew	cart	share
mole	stroke	huge	charm	snare
most	throat	juice	chart	spare
mow	throne	knew	dark	square
no	throw	mule	dart	stare
note	toad	mute	far	
oats	toast	new	farm	
old	toe	newt	guard	***er***
phone	told	rude	hard	clerk
poke	tone	rule	harm	fern
pole	tow	stew	jar	germ
post	vote	suit	large	her
quote	whole	threw	march	herd
roach	woe	through	mark	jerk
road	woke	true	park	merge
roam	yo-yo	tube	part	nerve
roast	yoke	tune	shark	perch
robe	zone	use	smart	perk
rode		view	spark	serve
role	**Long *u***	you	star	swerve
rope	blew	youth	start	term
rose	chew		tarp	verb
row	chute		tart	
scold	clue		war	

ir

birch
bird
birth
circle
dirt
fir
firm
first
flirt
girl
quirk
shirt
sir
skirt
squirm
squirt
stir
swirl
third
thirst
twirl
whirl

or

born
chord
chore
core
corn
dorm
for
force
ford
fork
form

fort
horn
horse
more
ore
porch
pork
port
score
shore
short
snore
sore
sort
sport
store
stork
storm
sword

ur

blur
burn
burp
burst
church
churn
curb
curse
curve
fur
hurry
hurt
nurse
purple
purse

surf
turn
urge

Special Vowel Sounds

aw as in paw

aw
awe
bawl
claw
crawl
dawn
draw
fawn
flaw
hawk
jaw
law
lawn
pawn
raw
saw
shawl
straw
thaw
yawn

ow as in cow

brow
brown
clown
cow
crowd
crown
down

drown
flower
frown
gown
how
howl
now
owl
plow
powder
power
shower
towel
tower
town
vow
vowel
wow